D1214357

The Indianapolis 500

Michael Dregni

Capstone Press

MINNEAPOLIS

Printed in the United States of America.

Capstone Press • 2440 Fernbrook Lane • Minneapolis, MN 55447

Editorial Director   John Coughlan
Managing Editor   John Martin
Copy Editor   Theresa Early
Editorial Assistant   Michelle Wood

Library of Congress Cataloging-in-Publication Data

Dregni, Michael, 1961-
   The Indianapolis 500 / Michael Dregni.
      p. cm.--
   Includes bibliographical references and index.
   ISBN 1-56065-205-5
   1. Indianapolis Speedway Race--Juvenile literature.
[1. Indianapolis Speedway Race.]   I. Title. II. Title:
Indianapolis Five Hundred. III. Series
GV1033.5.I55D74   1994
796.7'2'06877252--dc20   93-44567
                                          CIP
                                          AC

Table of Contents

Chapter 1

A Look at the Indianapolis 500

Auto racing is a sport of speed and spectacle and danger. One auto race is faster, more spectacular, and more dangerous than all the rest. It's the Indianapolis 500—the Super Bowl of auto racing and the World Series of Indy car racing.

The Indianapolis 500 is held each spring on Memorial Day weekend. Racers drive 500 miles (804 kilometers) on the world famous Indianapolis Motor Speedway in Indianapolis, Indiana.

On race day, the Speedway is full of brightly colored race cars, famous racing drivers, and a crowd of more than 500,000 auto racing fans.

More than 30 million people throughout the
world watch the race on television.

Before the start of the 1989 Indianapolis 500, racing crews crowd around the drivers on the starting grid.

Chapter 2

The History of the Indianapolis 500

The first automobile races took place in the United States around 1900. These races were run at county fairgrounds or on country roads.

In 1904, the Vanderbilt Cup races were first held in New York. The crowds of spectators grew every year, but they were soon banned by the state governor because of a series of deadly crashes.

Officials looked for a way to make racing more safe. They decided to build a racetrack that would take racing off the public roads.

And so the Indianapolis Motor Speedway was born.

"Eat My Dust"

Cars were heavy machinery in the days of the first Indy 500. Cars like the early Millers and Duesenbergs were like monstrous farm tractors.

To be a race car driver, you had to be strong. Gear shifts needed a muscular arm. Clutches needed a strong leg. And you had to use all of your strength to turn the car through corners.

Drivers had to be tough, as well. Indy drivers were fierce competitors. Some drivers hid away bolts or an extra wrench to throw at other drivers. One driver was known to carry a broom, which he held in the dirt to kick up dust.

When these tactics failed, a driver might bump another off the track. In those days, there was a lot more to racing than driving fast.

The first Indianapolis 500 race was held on May 30, 1911. The winner, Ray Harroun, averaged just 74.6 miles (120 kilometers) per hour–not very fast by today's standards.

Historical Highlights

• In the second Indy 500, in 1912, Ralph DePalma was in the lead. One and a half laps from the end, the engine of his German-built Mercedes blew up. DePalma jumped out. He and his mechanic pushed the car to the finish line. He didn't win, but he did finish—in 11th place!

• In 1966, Al Stein built an Indy car with two Porsche engines. One engine was in front to drive the front wheels, one was in back for the rear wheels.

• In 1967, STP ran a turbine car. It used a jet turbine engine from a helicopter, instead of a V-8 engine. It almost won.

• In 1985, driver Danny Sullivan was leading the race when he spun out at 200 miles (321 kilometers) per hour. He was just in front of second-place Mario Andretti. Miraculously, Sullivan came back to win. And Andretti finished second.

Chapter 3

Indy Cars

An Indy race car looks nothing like a car made for highways and roads. Every part is made for racing.

The Chassis

The **chassis** is the frame of the car. An Indy car chassis must be between 190 inches (482 centimeters) and 195 inches (495 centimeters) long. It must weigh 1550 pounds (703 kilograms) or less.

Some Indy car chassis makers are Lola, March, and Penske.

The Body

The body includes the **cockpit**, where the driver sits during a race. The **footwell** extends out into the **nose**. Behind the cockpit is the 40-gallon (151-liter) **fuel cell**. Behind the fuel cell is the engine. The body walls have to be both very strong and light.

The Wings

Attached to the front of the nose are the front wings. At the back of the chassis are the rear wings. As wind hits the wings, it creates **downforce**. This improves the car's traction.

Tires

Tires for Indy cars are very wide. Tires for dry races are smooth. Tires for rainy days have grooves to channel the water. The front tires are narrower than the rear tires, making it easier for the car to turn.

Engines

The engines of Indy cars have six or eight cylinders. They are very powerful. An Indy

Driver Arie Luyendyk sits in the cockpit of his Indy car.

engine will last for only about one race before it wears out and needs to be rebuilt.

Most of the engines used in the Indianapolis 500 use **turbochargers**. A turbocharger uses the car's exhaust gases to force more air/fuel mixture into the engine. A car can go faster when it burns more of the mixture.

This shot of an Indy car shows the long, slender body, the flat wings, and the fat tires.

GASOLINE ALLEY

The entrance to Gasoline Alley–the garage area where mechanics work hard to keep the cars in top running condition.

Chapter 4
The Brickyard

Carl Fisher, James Allison, Arthur Newby, and Frank Wheeler built the Indianapolis Motor Speedway.

The 2.5-mile (4-kilometer) track first opened on August 19, 1909. At that time the track was made of crushed stone and tar. But after many accidents, the management ruled the track unsafe.

Fisher immediately started workers paving the track. They used 3,200,000 bricks. This new track was much safer. It cost $200,000, a huge amount of money at that time.

The new track was nicknamed the Brickyard.

Pit stops at Indy must be quick and smooth.

It opened in May 1910. On May 30, 1911, the
first Indianapolis 500-mile race was run. The
race drew 90,000 fans and became an instant
success.

Beginning in 1937, parts of the track were
covered with asphalt. By 1976, asphalt covered
over all the original bricks except for a 36-inch
(91-centimeter) strip at the starting line.

The Indianapolis Motor Speedway is made

up of two long straightaways and two short straightaways. The "straights" are connected by four banked corners.

But there's more to winning at Indy than just driving around the track. To win the Indianapolis 500, a driver must have a clever racing strategy. The car must last the whole distance without breaking down. Each **pit stop** must be smooth and fast. And the team must know how to get the most out of their car.

A straightaway at the Indianapolis Motor Speedway

Chapter 5

The Race

To race in the Indianapolis 500, drivers must qualify. They must drive a fast enough **time trial.** A time trial is simple. The driver makes four laps around the two-and-a-half mile course, alone on the track. Each driver gets three chances to earn a starting position.

Hundreds of drivers enter the time trials. Only the 33 fastest drivers race in the Indianapolis 500.

Starting Positions

For the actual race, the cars are lined up on the **starting grid**.

The driver who has the fastest qualifying time

starts the race in **pole position**, or front inside position on the starting grid. This gives the driver a chance to get the "hole shot," for a quick lead in the first turn.

"Start Your Engines"

At the starting line, the drivers wait for the call, "Gentlemen, start your engines!" With the engines warmed up, they make one pace lap of the track behind the **pace car**.

The pace lap lets the cars gradually build speed. No passing or changing position is allowed. After the pace car finishes the lap, it drives off the track. The race referee waves the green flag, and the race begins.

Indy racers fly down the track at such high speeds that their cars push the air aside. This creates an air pocket directly behind the cars. Racers often drive close to the car in front of them, because driving within this air pocket lets them go faster. This style of driving is called **drafting**.

Indy cars sprint down the straightaways. Sometimes they reach speeds of 235 miles (378 kilometers) per hour.

The pace car leads the first lap of the Indianapolis 500.

For the turns, they ease off the gas. They brake, or even shift gears to slow down.

Each lap, drivers duel for position in the pack.

The Indy Pit Stop

The pit stop is when the car gets more fuel and fresh tires. Every car must make several pit stops. The rule of the pit stop is simple. Make it quick.

With the stopwatch running, here's how a typical pit stop works:

Seconds 1-5

The Indy car comes into its pit area and stops.

Four crew members wait with air-powered wrenches and new tires. Wearing fireproof gloves and suits, the crew members dash to their stations. They wait for the air jacks to lift the car. As soon as the car is raised, the crew begins to take off the hot tires.

The fueler pulls a fuel line from behind the pit wall. It is plugged into the car's gas intake. The fueler wears a helmet and eye shields.

The driver is given a plastic bottle filled with water or another drink.

Seconds 6-10

The four wheels are unbolted with a whirr of the wrenches.

Other crew members hand off new wheels and tires from behind the pit wall. They are hoisted into place. The wrenches buzz again as the new tires are bolted on. The old tires are carried out of the way.

The first seconds of an Indy pit stop

During the pit stop every second is important.

Seconds 11-15

The fuel tank is full and the hose is reeled in.

The crew releases the air jack and the car drops to the ground.

Crew members dash behind the car to help push-start it. This keeps the car from stalling.

The driver checks for any other cars in the pit area, guns the engine, and lets out the clutch.

The Indy car blasts out of the pit, onto the track, and back into the race.

Running for the Checkered Flag

It all comes down to one final lap. Coming around that last corner of the Brickyard, the Indy cars are packed together. Only inches separate the wheels. After 500 miles (804 kilometers), it is the inches that count.

Finally they hit the last straightaway. The drivers hit a top speed of about 235 miles (378 kilometers) per hour. The noise is so loud you would think that everyone in Indianapolis could hear the race.

The cheering crowd jumps to its feet. The driver in the lead weaves slightly, side to side, to keep the second-place car from passing.

Just an instant away from the finish line, the second car makes its move. But the lead driver blocks it. The crowd roars like a lion. The race is won!

Emerson Fittipaldi after winning the 1993 Indianapolis 500

Chapter 6

Famous Drivers

The drivers of the Indy 500 are well known around the world.

Some of the most famous American Indy racers are Mario Andretti, Al Unser, Jr., and Danny Sullivan. There are also famous drivers from around the globe. Emerson Fittipaldi comes from Brazil. Roberto Guerrero and Arie Luyendyk come from Europe.

There is one great hero of the Indy 500. That man is A.J. Foyt. Foyt won his first Indy 500 in 1961. He has come back to race at Indy more than 25 times. He was still winning a share of the prize money in the 1990s. He has won four Indy 500 races, more than any other driver.

The rollover hoop (above) and six-point seatbelts (below) protect the driver in the event of a crash or rollover.

Chapter 7
Safety

S ince Indy racing started, speeds have steadily increased. So have the risks. Drivers now take many safety measures to ensure that racing remains safe.

Safety Equipment

On the Indy car just behind the driver's head is the **rollover hoop**. This horseshoe-shaped hoop is made of a very strong and light material. It's there in case the car rolls over in a crash. This hoop would keep the driver's head from scraping the pavement.

Six-point seatbelts hold the driver in place.

The need for safety equipment: Nigel Mansell crashing at 180 miles (290 kilometers) per hour

An Indy car is carried away after a crash.

They prevent the rider from being thrown out of the car in a crash.

Engineers have added special screws, bolts, and nuts that will pop open when hit. In a crash, the car "breaks" apart. The shock of the crash goes into breaking up the car. The sturdy cockpit holds together and keeps the driver safe.

Safety Clothing

Driving suits, socks, gloves, and even underwear are all made of a fire-resistant cloth called Nomex.

Drivers also wear a fireproof hood called a **balaclava**. A balaclava looks like a ski mask.

Extra precautions are taken to prevent fire. The methanol that Indy cars burn is held in a fuel cell. The fuel cell is very hard to break. It can even withstand the impact of a bullet.

Driving helmet and gloves on fireproof blanket of Nomex

Actor Paul Newman watches his team compete at the 1991 Indianapolis 500.

Chapter 8

How Much
Does It Cost?

Racing is expensive. Most cars are owned by one person. Indy owners include famous racer Roger Penske and actor and driver Paul Newman.

Owners pay for more than just the cars, equipment, and transportation. They must also pay the racing team for their work. The team includes drivers, mechanics, and pit crew.

The costs of the Indianapolis 500 cars and equipment can add up quickly. A team needs at least one extra chassis, in case something breaks. They need one engine to qualify and

Sponsors give money to racing teams in exchange for advertising. The car above is sponsored by Scotch™.

practice. They need another engine to race. They need several sets of wheels and several sets of tires. And they need equipment to haul the cars and spare parts to the track.

It adds up to at least $2.5 million. It could cost as much as $5 million. To help pay the

bills, the owner looks for **sponsors**. A sponsor
is a person or a company that helps pay for the
race team. In exchange, the sponsor gets its
name on the Indy race car and on the driver's
racing suits.

Indy cars take advantage of the latest technology.
Above, a Chevrolet Indy V-8. Below, Team Molson's
metal alloy chassis.

Chapter 9

Indy High Tech

In the early years of Indy racing, a mechanic rode in the car during the race. If the car broke down, the mechanic hopped out and worked on the car on the spot. Today, racing teams use computers to test and control Indy cars from the pit area.

Computers in Race Cars

The modern Indy cars have several computer sensors in their engines. The sensors send information to a computer in the pit.

With these sensors, the crew can tell if the tires are running too hot. The computer can also tell whether the engine is producing all the horsepower it should.

The crew uses the computer to adjust the settings on the car. They can, for example, adjust the amount of fuel flowing into the engine even while the car is racing around the track!

Glossary

balaclava–a snug-fitting, fire-resistant hood worn under the driver's helmet

chassis–the framework of a car, including the wheels, axles, and parts for mounting the engine

cockpit–the place in a car where the driver sits

downforce–the force that presses a car to the ground and is produced by air passing over and under the moving car

drafting–following closely behind a speeding car to take advantage of the front car's pushing aside the air in its path

footwell–the section of an Indy car where the drivers place their feet

fuel cell–a container for holding fuel, usually metal or plastic with a rubber bladder inside

nose–the cone-shaped front of an Indy car

pace car–a car that leads the racing cars around the track before the beginning of a race

pit stop–to leave a race temporarily for repairs or fuel

pole position–the position on the inside of the front row at the beginning of a race, awarded to the car with the best qualifying time

rollover hoop–a horseshoe-shaped metal frame behind the driver that prevents injury in the case of a rollover

sponsor–a company or individual who provides the financial support for a racing team

starting grid–the lineup of cars as they start a race

time trials–these races determine who qualifies to race in the Indianapolis 500. Racers drive the course alone for the fastest lap times.

turbocharger–a device driven by a car's exhaust gases that forces extra air and fuel into the engine for added power and speed

To Learn More

About the Indianapolis 500:

Andretti, Michael. *Michael Andretti at Indianapolis*. New York: Simon & Schuster, 1992.

Murphy, Jim. *The Indy 500*. New York: Clarion, 1983.

About Indy Cars:

Robinson, Scott. *Indy Cars*. New York: Crestwood House, 1988.

Rubel, David. *How to Drive an Indy Race Car*. Santa Fe, NM: John Muir, 1992.

Sullivan, George. *Racing Indy Cars*. New York: Cobblehill, 1992.

Wilkinson, Sylvia. *Champ Cars*. Chicago: Childrens Press, 1982.

Index

Wickliffe Elementary School
1821 Lincoln Rd.
Wickliffe, OH 44092